Open a Book!

By David Messick

Featuring the Rainbow Puppets

Illustrated by Liu Light

D1366931

To Marcy

Open a Book!

© 2018 / All Rights Reserved
Text David Messick
Illustrations Liu Light
Puppet images Rainbow Productions, Inc.

Adapted from the Song "Open A Book" by David Messick

ISBN: **978-0-692-18681-7**

Printed in PRC.
Second Printing
Rainbow Puppet Publications
18 Easthill Court
Hampton, Virginia 23664

www.rainbowpuppets.com
info@rainbowpuppets.com

Rainbow Puppet Productions, Inc.is a non-profit, educational, entertainment company

Thank you to all of the artists who have shared their gifts with us. They include:

Kathie Davis: Sea Horse, Sea Star

Christine Frank: Fiddler Crabs, Mother Goose

Jill Harrington: Astronaut in Blue, Fish, Gonzorgo, Grumio, Humpty, Mary Peake, Mermaid,
Moon, Powhatan, Red Riding Hood, Stars, Students, Sun, Tuskegee Airmen, Wolf

Laura Huff: Abraham Lincoln, Aladdin, Captain Mick, Eleanor Roosevelt,
Parasaurolophus, Patrick Henry

Frank Lakus: Electric Eel

Regina Smith: Astronaut in White, Costumes

Helen Spaetzel: Gingerbread Men

Jason Wiedel: Props

Designed by Lynn Mangosing

Photos by Judy Lowery

Special thanks to Curtis Johnson, Ruth Manlove, Traci Massie, and Rose West at Optima Health; Jim and
Linda Haas at the Academy of Dance; Julia MacPherson and Marty Staton, two terrific children's librarians
and supporters and, of course, Stephanie and David Messick, Sr. (mom and dad).

If you've got a question
and need an answer
right away...

Open a Book!

Open a Book!

Seeking adventure and
your friends can't come and play?

Open a Book!
Open a Book!

You can find so many things to do.

Anytime you

And you're sure to learn a thing or two…

Open a Book!

So, won't you take a look
inside a history book?

See Mary Peake teach
underneath a tree.

The Wright Brothers believed
if they took time to read...

their plan to make an airplane
would succeed!

You can find a house made out of candy.

See a dinosaur who likes to roar.

Travel to a beach
that's bright and sandy.

Maybe there's
a mermaid near the shore.

You can even dive...

in the ocean wide.

Join Aladdin as he takes

a magic carpet ride.

Find fun and adventure...

Mother Goose and Nursery Rhymes.

Open a Book!
Open a Book!

Meet famous people as you travel back in time…

**Open a Book!
Open a Book!**

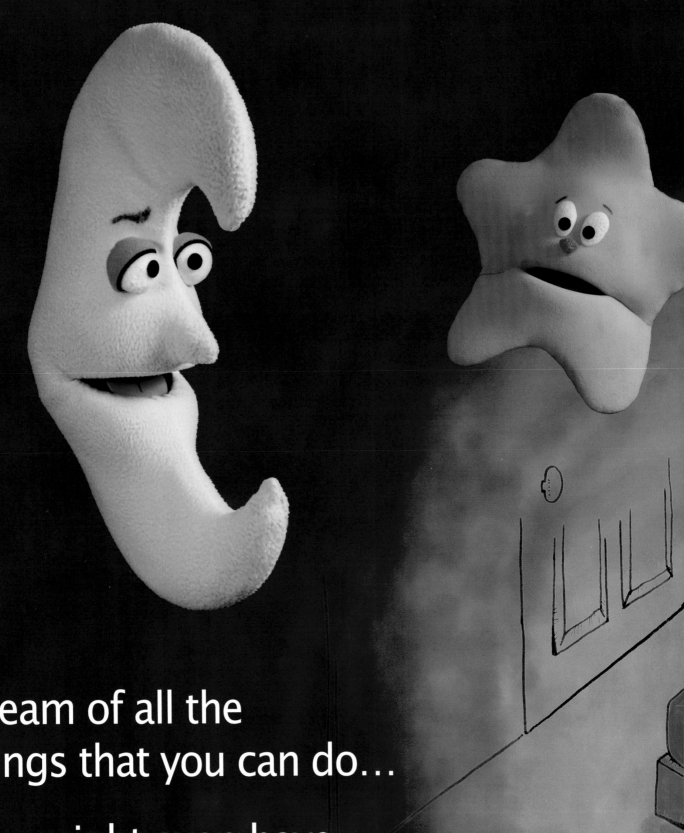

Dream of all the things that you can do…

You might even have your dreams come true.

Anytime that you...

Open a Book!

Rainbow uses many different types of puppets...

James is using a hand puppet. James can open and close his hand to make the sun talk and wish you a great day.

David is working a human arm puppet. He uses one hand to move Mother Goose's mouth and another to make her wing wave at you.

Josh is holding a rod puppet. This style was probably first used in Egypt and India. It gets the name from the rod or stick that is used to make it move. This one is a sea star.

Michael is operating our giant marionette puppet. Sometimes they are called "string puppets." This guy does a terrific moon walk.

SWAN

Shadow Puppets

WOLF

BIRD or BUTTERFLY

You can make shadow puppets of your own. We think shadow puppets were the first puppets ever presented. You can use a flashlight or other lamp to make the shadows. We'd love to hear about the show you create!

You can find more activities and learn about the characters in this book at **www.rainbowpuppets.com**.

Alyssa and Wesley operate human arm puppets.

David Messick is the founder of Rainbow Puppet Productions. As a writer and composer, he has created dozens of original children's musicals. As a director and performer, he has worked with legendary artists like Mickey Rooney, Carol Channing, and Geoffrey Holder. He's produced internationally-recognized television commercials and worked on development projects for the Oprah Winfrey Show and the Disney Channel. He and his wife Marcy have been blessed with two amazing boys...Joshua and Luke.
www.davidmessick.com

Liu Light is an illustrator, writer, and art book maker currently based in Richmond, Virginia. A graduate of Virginia Commonwealth University, Light is involved with a number of community organizations for emerging marginalized artists. Notable collaborations include work with Shout Mouse Press and 3 Moons along with a number of east coast Art Book Fairs and Zinefests.
liulight.tumbler.com

Rainbow Puppet Productions presents programs that entertain, enlighten, and educate children and their families. In additional to performing at hundreds of libraries and schools across the country, they have been seen at the Smithsonian National Air and Space Museum, the American Museum of Natural History in New York, and Washington DC's National Theater. They are the 2018 Sunburst Performing Artists of the Year, recognized for consistently delivering "highly choreographed and well-planned performances that engage audiences with their exceptional energy and charisma."
www.rainbowpuppets.com

Rainbow Puppeteers include James Cooper; Wesley Huff; Alyssa Jones; David, Marcy, and Joshua Messick; and Michael Singleton.